TEAMMATES

MICHAEL JORDAN ★ SCOTTIE PIPPEN

BILL GUTMAN

THE MILLBROOK PRESS
BROOKFIELD, CONNECTICUT

Photographs courtesy of AP/Wide World Photos: pp. 7, 18, 23, 48, 63, 74, 84, 88, 99, 105; New Hanover County Public Library, Tidewater Collection: p. 12; Seth Poppel Yearbook Archives: p. 30; NBA Photos: pp. 36 (© Nathaniel S. Butler), 42 (© Scott Cunningham), 57 (© Scott Cunningham), 78 (© Barry Jarvinen), 93 (© Andy Hayt)

Library of Congress Cataloging-in-Publication Data
Gutman, Bill.
Teammates : Michael Jordan and Scottie Pippen / Bill Gutman.
p. cm.
Summary: A dual biography of two star players for the Chicago Bulls, describing their separate basketball careers and how they have performed as teammates.
ISBN 0-7613-0420-7 (lib. bdg.)
1. Jordan, Michael, 1963-   —Juvenile literature. 2. Pippen, Scottie—Juvenile literature. 3. Basketball players—United States—Biography—Juvenile literature. 4. Chicago Bulls (Basketball team)—Juvenile literature. [1. Jordan, Michael, 1963-   . 2. Pippen, Scottie. 3. Basketball players. 4. Afro-Americans—Biography. 5. Chicago Bulls (Basketball team)] I. Title.
GV884.J67G888   1998   796.323'092'277311—dc21
[B]   98-3030 CIP AC

Published by The Millbrook Press, Inc.
2 Old New Milford Road
Brookfield, Connecticut 06804

CONTENTS

INTRODUCTION

They fit together perfectly, like fingers in a glove. One is the universally acclaimed greatest player in the history of his sport. The other is so good at every aspect of the game that there is virtually no way to check him. Together they have enjoyed five National Basketball Association championships. This is what having Michael Jordan and Scottie Pippen playing side by side can do for a team—in this case, the Chicago Bulls.

In a way, however, many fans didn't really appreciate how important the two players were to each other until the 1996–1997 NBA playoffs. The reason was simple. Michael Jordan was such an incredible player that he was often perceived as a one-man team, a superstar with a supporting cast.

Yet when the Bulls set an NBA record with 72 victories in 1995–1996, then followed it with 69 wins in 1996–1997, it became apparent that Michael was not the only reason.

Scottie Pippen's stellar all-around game came to the fore in the 1997 playoffs. In the first game of the Bulls' series with the Atlanta Hawks, it was Scottie who hit a clutch three-point shot to win the game 100–97. Afterward, Jordan corrected those who had doubted Scottie's ability to come up big with the game on the line. "I have never doubted Scottie in the clutch," Michael said. "You guys [in the media] do. I always felt he could make the big shot, and he has."

Scottie's contributions might not have been as spectacular as Michael's, but they could no longer be ignored. As the Bulls won their fifth championship in seven years with a 90–86 victory in the sixth game, it was once again the two superstars who made it possible. Michael scored 39, while Scottie had 23 as well as playing his great game at both ends of the court. The dynamic duo had scored 62 of the Bulls' 90 points. And when Jordan was given the award as the Most Valuable Player in the finals, he quickly called Scottie over and insisted that Scottie help him hold it aloft. And he told the basketball world in no uncertain terms, "This is as much [Scottie's] award as it is mine. I want to share it with him."

Chicago Bulls teammates Michael Jordan (left) and Scottie Pippen hoist the trophy after beating the Utah Jazz to win the 1997 NBA championship, their fifth in seven years.

Despite their multifaceted skills, Michael and Scottie are not carbon copies of one another. Jordan is the game's greatest scorer, a player capable of producing 40- or even 50-point nights if his team needs a big lift. His ability to score on a variety of drives, fallaway jumpers, and three-pointers is almost uncanny. When he is in the "zone" he can take the entire team on his back and propel it to victory.

A very solid scorer in his own right, Pippen possesses all-league skills in every phase of the game. It is the incredible versatility of both athletes that has made them perennial All-Stars and the Bulls a team so difficult to beat.

Michael is 6 feet 6 inches (198 centimeters) tall and Scottie is 6 feet 7 inches (200 centimeters) tall, yet both can bring the ball up court with the dexterity of a smaller point guard. Both are outstanding defensive players and can rebound against much taller foes. Either is as capable of throwing a brilliant pass as making a brilliant shot. In short, there is virtually nothing on the basketball court that this pair of superstars can't do.

The two have been teammates since the 1987–1988 season, the year Scottie joined the Bulls from tiny Central Arkansas University. Michael had come to the team three years earlier after a star-studded tenure at the University of North Carolina. He was

already a superstar when Scottie joined the team. It took a few years for Scottie's game to approach Michael's. But when it finally happened, the Bulls became an elite team and have been one ever since.

1 CAROLINA ALL THE WAY

What is it that separates a good basketball player from a great one? Talent is certainly a starting point. But natural ability can take a player only so far. There comes a time when that player must harness every ounce of his talent, then go deep down inside himself and find something beyond that, something extra special. To become great takes dedication, desire, perseverance, and a huge amount of old-fashioned hard work.

Just like talent, those qualities also have to be developed. An individual usually has to have help—from a caring family, a dedicated coach, and solid friends. There's really no way to predict which athletes will find these special qualities.

When Michael Jeffrey Jordan was born on February 17, 1963, no one knew that he would be the greatest basketball player in the world. Not even his parents. James and Delores Jordan were just happy that their third son was healthy. They were also concerned about raising their growing family, which would number three boys and two girls, in a safe place.

Michael was born in Brooklyn, New York. Brooklyn is one of the five boroughs of New York City. As in many large cities, the streets of Brooklyn could be tough. Crime, drugs, and violence were not uncommon. The Jordans decided they didn't want their children to grow up there. Shortly after Michael was born, the family moved to Wilmington, North Carolina.

Wilmington was a laid-back, sleepy seaport town of 56,000 people. The Jordans felt that it would be a good place to raise their children, and they quickly began setting an example of hard work and responsibility. James Jordan worked as a mechanic at a General Electric plant in Wilmington in 1967. He worked his way up to dispatcher, then foreman, and finally to supervisor. Delores Jordan became a teller at the United Carolina Bank in Wilmington. Eventually, she became the head of customer relations at the bank's downtown branch.

It took Michael awhile to understand his parents' work ethic. At first, he was a sometimes lazy

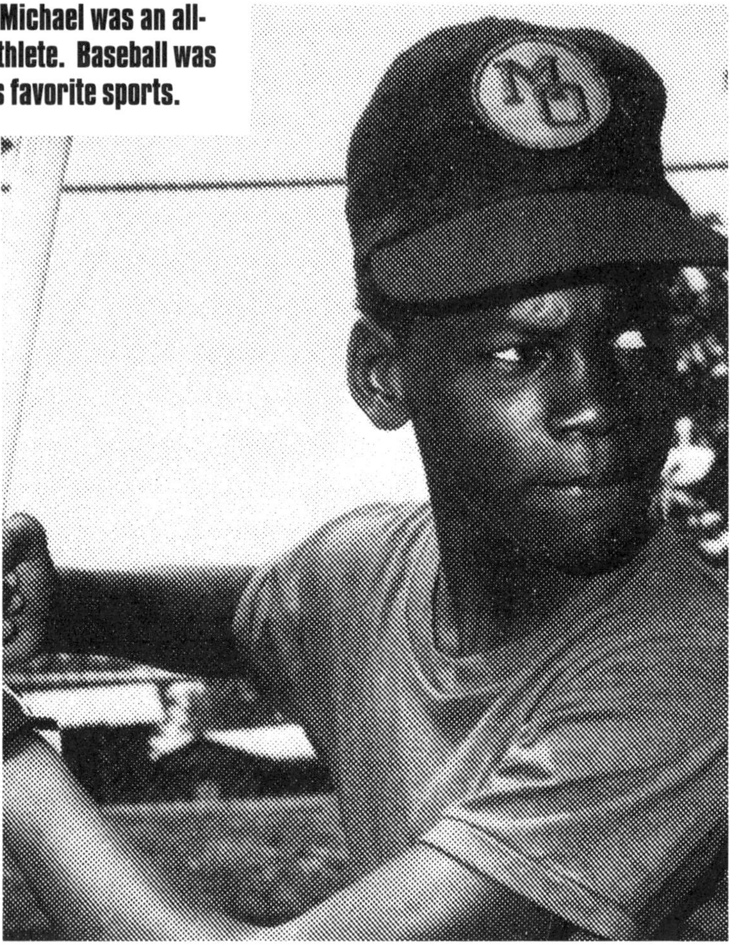

As a kid, Michael was an all-around athlete. Baseball was one of his favorite sports.

athlete who couldn't compete with his older brother, Larry. In fact, baseball was Michael's best sport when he was young. At age 12, he was named the top baseball player in his league. Even though he was very thin then, he could throw a baseball hard. At D.C. Virgo Junior High, Michael also played basketball and football.

When Michael reached Laney High School as a 10th grader, he was 5 feet 11 inches (180 centimeters). That made him 2 inches (5 centimeters) taller than his father and 3 inches (8 centimeters) taller than his brother Larry. But since no one in the Jordan family had ever topped 6 feet (183 centimeters), he didn't think he would grow much more. And while he was already a good basketball player, he wasn't a great one. He certainly hadn't thought about playing in the NBA.

Shortly after entering Laney, three things happened that led to a change in attitude and new goals for Michael. As a sophomore, he was the starting point guard on the junior varsity (JV) team. Toward the end of the season the word was that one of the JV players would be brought up to the varsity. Michael thought he would get the call, but a much taller player was chosen.

"I made up my mind right then and there that this would never happen to me again," Michael said. "From that point on, I began working harder than ever on my basketball skills."

It was his newfound dedication that led to Michael's second lesson. He began practicing so much that he was cutting classes and angering his teachers. That's when his father stepped in. When Michael told his father that his goal was to go to college to play basketball, James Jordan said sternly

that there was no way Michael would get there if he kept cutting classes.

Michael learned to set priorities. Schoolwork came first. But he still managed to practice basketball more than anyone else. Later, he would often credit his parents for his ultimate success. "Who knows what would have happened if my father hadn't talked to me," he said. "I was lucky enough to have parents who cared. They always gave me guidance and at the same time taught me to work hard."

Between Michael's sophomore and junior years at Laney, something amazing happened. Michael grew suddenly, gaining 4 inches (10 centimeters) by the time he returned to school in the fall. He was now 6 feet 3 inches (190 centimeters). Even his father couldn't believe it. "It was almost as if he willed himself taller," James Jordan said.

From that point, Michael began growing quickly as a basketball player, too. He gave up football so he could concentrate more on basketball. Then, during his senior year, he gave up baseball. He was down to one sport, and he started an amazing basketball practice routine that would become a way of life.

Even though he was on the varsity team, Michael would practice with the Laney JV team from 5:30 to 7:00 P.M. He would do all the drills and the

exhausting wind sprints at the end. Then, he would stay for varsity practice from 7:00 to 9:00 P.M. Fred Lynch, who had coached him in junior high and was now a Laney assistant, saw the way Michael pursued basketball. "Beginning his junior year, Michael was the hardest working athlete I'd ever seen," Lynch said. "He'd also be in the gym on Saturdays and Sundays, playing all day long. There may have been other kids with nearly as much talent as Michael, but they just didn't want to pay dues the way he did."

Michael also acquired other traits at that time which would serve him well in the pros. "One thing he always demanded was that the other players go as hard as he did," Fred Lynch explained. "From that standpoint, he was a pusher. It stemmed from his being so competitive and hating to lose."

By the time his junior year ended, Michael was already being recruited by the University of North Carolina. North Carolina, under Coach Dean Smith, had one of the top basketball programs in the country. And that summer, Michael attended the Five Star Basketball Camp, a place where many top high school prospects gather to show their skills and to learn. It didn't take long for him to show everyone there that he was a budding force.

"The first time he took a jump shot he got up so high it was like there was no defender," said

Tom Konchalski, whose job it was to evaluate the high school talent.

During his week at the camp, Michael excelled in every phase of the game. He won five trophies for individual excellence and was invited to stay a second week. All the hours of practice and hard work were beginning to pay off. Michael was clearly the best player at the camp, winning four more trophies the second week. Now, even Michael realized how good he had become. "Nobody knew me till I went up there, and I was scared," he said, later. "But I played my best ever at the camp and really got some recognition. It was the turning point of my life."

Soon after, Michael visited the North Carolina campus at Chapel Hill. He liked what he saw and during his senior year at Laney High, he signed to attend the University of North Carolina in the fall of 1981. He would receive a full scholarship. But before he went to Chapel Hill he had to finish high school. That meant one more basketball season.

Even with his college plans set, Michael didn't rest. He worked harder than ever and pushed his teammates to play their best. He was now 6 feet 5 inches (195 centimeters) and his height helped him average 27.8 points and 12 rebounds a game. He had become an incredible player, and, at college, he would have a chance to show the entire nation how good he was.

Michael graduated from Laney High in the spring of 1981. That fall, he entered the University of North Carolina at Chapel Hill and would be joining one of the best collegiate basketball teams in the country. Coach Smith had junior forward James Worthy and sophomore center Sam Perkins, both considered potential All-Americans, in his starting lineup. Senior Jimmy Black started at point guard, and sophomore Matt Doherty was in the small forward spot. There was one spot open—shooting guard.

Just before the team's first game against Kansas, Coach Smith named Michael the fifth starter, an unusual move, since Michael was a freshman. "I didn't know I was starting until I saw my name on the board," he said, "and believe me, I was nervous."

Michael missed his first shot, a medium jumper. But the second time his team, the Tar Heels, had the ball, he took a baseline jumper over a pair of Kansas defenders and swished it! It was the first two points of the game. The Michael Jordan era had begun. North Carolina won the game, 74–67, with Michael scoring 12 points, hitting five of ten from the field and two of two from the line.

Two games later he went over 20 points for the first time. He was fitting in beautifully. And by the first week in January, the Tar Heels were a perfect 10–0 and the number-one ranked team in the country. North Carolina would finish the 1981–1982

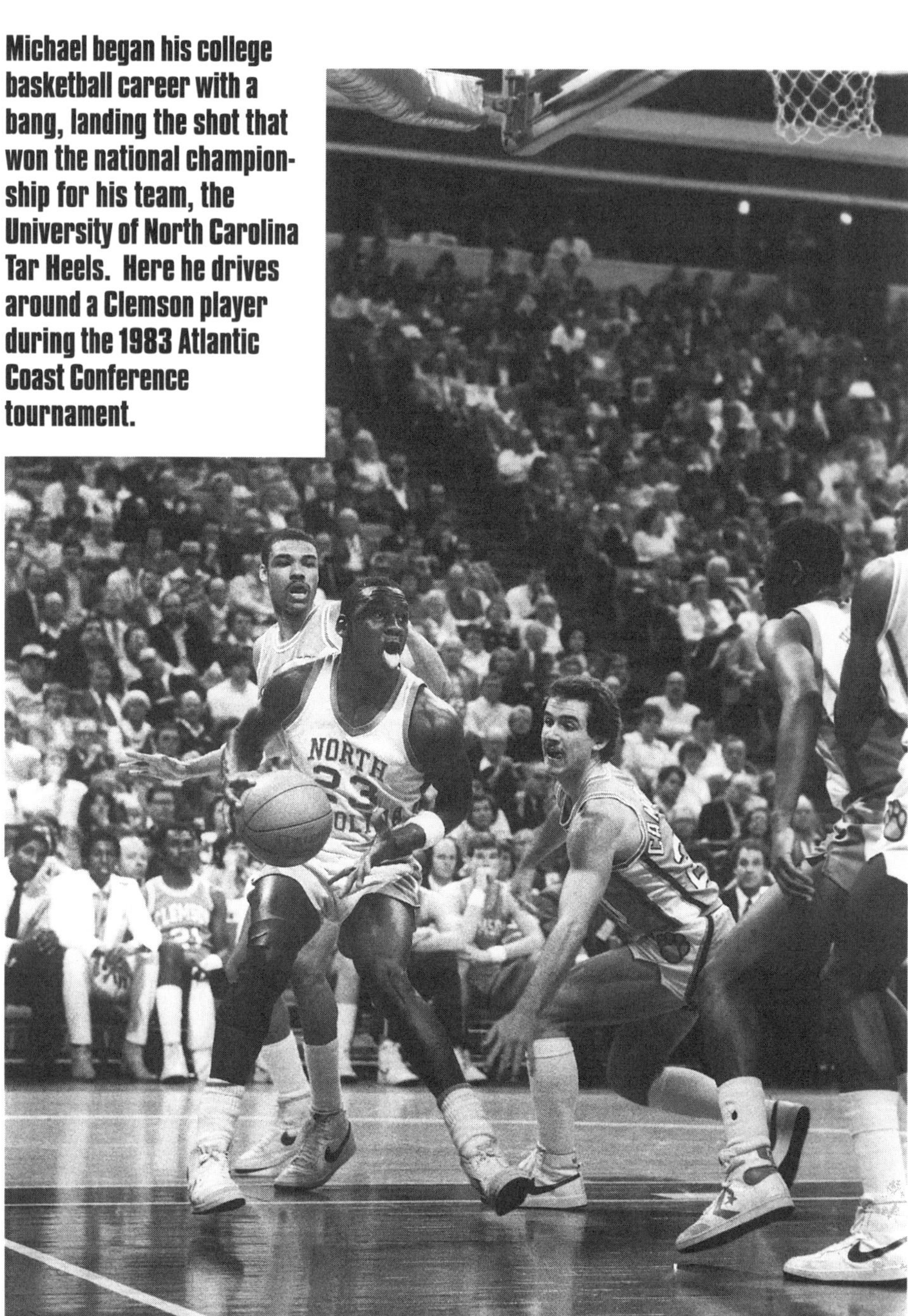

Michael began his college basketball career with a bang, landing the shot that won the national champion-ship for his team, the University of North Carolina Tar Heels. Here he drives around a Clemson player during the 1983 Atlantic Coast Conference tournament.

season with just two losses and was the number-one seed overall in the NCAA tournament to determine the national champion. Here again, the Michael Jordan legend was about to grow.

Despite some close calls, Carolina made it to the title game. There, the Tar Heels would be meeting the Hoyas of Georgetown University. Georgetown also had a freshman star, 7-foot-tall (213-centimeter) center Patrick Ewing.

The game settled into a real struggle, with Georgetown taking a 32–31 halftime lead. The second half was just as close. Finally, Carolina had a 62–61 lead with just 1:19 left. Georgetown had the ball and worked it slowly. They wanted to go inside to Ewing, but the Tar Heels had him boxed in. Finally, with just 32 seconds left, Hoya guard "Sleepy" Floyd hit a 12-foot jumper to give Georgetown the lead at 62–61. Carolina called a time out to regroup.

When play resumed, the Tar Heels wanted to get the ball to Worthy, who already had 28 points. But the Hoya defense was watching him closely. They continued to work it. Jimmy Black had the ball and suddenly whipped a pass to Michael, who was on the left baseline, 16 feet (5 meters) from the hoop. With 17 seconds left and with the national championship on the line, Michael calmly went up for a jump shot. "I had a good feeling about it

when I let [the ball] go," he said, later. "But I didn't know for sure."

The ball floated in the air as both teams, the 61,000 fans at the Superdome in New Orleans, and millions more on television watched.

SWISH!

Michael had hit the biggest basket of his life. It gave North Carolina a 63–62 lead. And when Georgetown committed a turnover with just seconds left, the Tar Heels had won the national championship. The clutch basket by the freshman Michael Jordan is still known around Chapel Hill as, simply, "The Shot."

Michael had scored 16 points in the title game, second to Worthy's 28. And he led his team with 9 rebounds. For the season, he averaged 13.5 points in 34 games, shooting 53.4 percent from the field. His future was still ahead of him, but his legacy at North Carolina was already cemented . . . because of The Shot.

Now a celebrity, Michael settled in at the Chapel Hill campus. He knew the importance of his studies and was a solid B student. He had also chosen geography as his major field of study. Of course, Michael continued to practice basketball, even in the off-season.

James Worthy left North Carolina after his junior year to enter the NBA draft, and wouldn't be

part of the 1982–1983 team. But it was soon apparent that sophomore Michael Jordan would be able to pick up the slack. He was now at his full height of 6 feet 6 inches (198 centimeters) and was close to 200 pounds (90 kilograms).

Michael knew that just making The Shot in the title game the year before wouldn't allow him to glide through the rest of his college career. "I wanted to be recognized as a complete player," he said, "a guy who doesn't just come through at the last minute, but one who's there the entire game."

Though he was just a sophomore, Michael was attracting the attention of not only those in the collegiate ranks, but those looking for future pros, too. Bruce Dalrymple, the Georgia Tech coach, said Michael was "an incredible worker with an incredible amount of talent," adding: "His attitude is, 'you can push me or hit me, but I'm going to do what has to be done.' It shows on his face, and that's what makes Jordan so great."

Carolina won another Atlantic Coast Conference (ACC) title in 1982–1983, then lost in the NCAA regionals to Georgia. The team finished a fine season at 28–8. But it was Michael who really excelled. He averaged 20 points a game, with 5.5 rebounds, and shot 53.5 percent from the field. He was a consensus All-American and was then named College Basketball Player of the Year.

The 1983–1984 season was more of the same. Carolina had an excellent team that once again won the ACC championship and entered the NCAA Tournament with a 27–2 record. The team won its opening game with Temple, but then was upset by Indiana, 72–68, ending the Tar Heels' season.

Michael averaged 19.6 points a game, was again an All-American, and for the second straight year was named College Basketball Player of the Year. While there were those who scored more points, astute basketball observers felt that the North Carolina system made Michael a better all-around player. If he were at another school, he probably could have averaged close to 30 points a game.

"I think Dean Smith's system helped Michael," said his high school coach, Fred Lynch. "It teaches discipline and also tells a ballplayer if he doesn't play defense, he's not going to play. From that standpoint, it made Michael into a much more well-rounded ballplayer."

Now the question was: Would Michael return for his senior year? A number of Carolina players had left school early with Coach Smith's blessing, and he also suggested that Michael turn pro. Michael was leaning toward returning. He had always said that his goal was to graduate. On the other hand, there was little doubt that Michael was

Soon after Michael announced that he would not return for his senior year of college, he was drafted by the Chicago Bulls. Here he answers questions for reporters after signing a seven-year contract with the Bulls.

ready for the NBA. The coach felt that Michael could make a lot of money as a pro and that he should take the opportunity.

Finally, on May 5, 1984, Michael called a news conference at Chapel Hill to announce his intentions. He stepped to the microphone as everyone waited anxiously to hear what he would say. Sure enough, he announced that he was giving up his final year of college eligibility to turn pro.

"I don't owe the fans or alumni a last year at this university," he said. "I have to do what's best for me. If I owe anyone, it's my parents, who have put up with me for 20 years.

"Money plays a big part in each one of our lives. Who knows? I may not be around next year. I think it's better to start now. But this wasn't solely a financial decision. Here is a chance to move up to a higher level, make a better life for myself, and make me wiser about the life that is going on around me."

Michael had closed the book on a very important phase of his life and was ready to begin a new one. He had worked, learned, and provided thrills to many fans. Now he was ready to move on. No one could know then just what kind of impact he would have on the game of basketball in the years ahead.

2 FROM A TINY TOWN IN ARKANSAS

The town of Hamburg, Arkansas, could be described as one of those places in the middle of nowhere where everyone knows everyone else and not much changes. Hamburg was tiny; not the kind of place that was geared to produce a future NBA superstar. If a superstar were to come out of a small town like Hamburg, he would most likely have to do it almost by himself. That's why no one figured that Scottie Pippen would become a professional basketball player.

Maurice Scotty Pippen was born in Hamburg on September 25, 1965. (He later changed the "y" in Scotty to "ie.") The population of the town then was just 3,394 people. The population of the Pippen family was 14: mother, father, and 12 children. Scottie was the youngest son and last child born to Ethel and Preston Pippen. With such a large family to care for, Mrs. Pippen stayed at home. Mr. Pippen worked long hours at a local paper and plywood mill to provide for everyone. The hard work and the need for everyone to help made the family extremely close.

There weren't many activities in and around Hamburg. The town had two shirt factories, a lumber company, and the mill where Mr. Pippen worked. Family life centered around making a living, and being together. Although Scottie was the youngest, he was always included in family activities and was made to feel important by the older kids.

"My sisters would always have me do little things for them," Scottie remembered. "They would have me doing this and doing that, but always for a couple of dollars. I did it because I was one of those kids who always wanted to have a couple of dollars in my pocket."

Though Scottie was small and very thin as a boy, he began playing sports early. Baseball and basketball are sports that kids can play almost anywhere, and Hamburg was no exception. Almost all of the boys played. By the time Scottie was a teenager, sports took a good deal of his time.

"We used to play at the Pine Street courts," said his boyhood friend, Ron Martin. "It was when we were about 13 or 14. We played as late as we could, until this old man would run us off for making noise. When we played baseball, Scottie was on the Giants, I was on the A's."

Scottie remembers playing one-on-one "forever," saying that he and his friend Ron must have played a "million games."

Scottie was so into sports that he even played some football in junior high despite his thin frame. At that time, however, he wasn't an exceptional athlete. Yet by the time he entered high school, he had a goal. He had decided he wanted to play in the National Basketball Association. He didn't know that there would soon be a family crisis that might have ended his dream forever.

It happened shortly after Scottie began 10th grade in the fall of 1980. His father came home from another long workday at the paper mill. Suddenly, Mr. Pippen collapsed to the floor. He was rushed to the hospital by ambulance, where doctors learned that he had suffered a massive stroke. As a result, Scottie's father would be partially paralyzed and have to stay in a wheelchair.

Because Mr. Pippen couldn't work any longer, the family had to adjust. Now, everyone would have to pitch in more than ever. Though he was the youngest, Scottie talked about quitting school and getting a job. He wanted to do his part. But his mother and older siblings all urged him to stay in school. Most of them were already out of school and working. They could all help support the family. There was no need for Scottie to quit, they said. He took his family's advice.

Unlike Michael Jordan, who became an outstanding basketball player and top prospect while still in high school, Scottie was just average. He wasn't yet 6 feet (183 centimeters) tall when he entered Hamburg High, and he didn't even try out for the basketball team. He spent a year as a manager for the football team, carrying towels and water buckets. He wasn't an active member of the basketball team until his senior year of 1982–1983. That same year Michael Jordan was named College Basketball Player of the Year. No one outside of Hamburg, Arkansas, had even heard of Scottie Pippen.

As a senior, Scottie had grown to 6 feet 1 inch (185 centimeters), but was still very thin and weighed just 150 pounds (68 kilograms). Surprisingly, Scottie won the starting point guard job, mainly because he was consistent and didn't make many mistakes. "There was nothing special or flashy about him," said his coach, Donald Wayne. "People would ask me all the time why I was starting him."

Hamburg High didn't have a super team, and Scottie began to worry that he would not be able to continue with the game in college. Not a single college scout or recruiter came to see him play.

In tiny Hamburg, it would have been difficult for even an outstanding player to attract attention. An average player like Scottie simply didn't have a chance. Not knowing what else to do, he went to his coach and asked for help. Seeing Scottie's determination, Coach Wayne called his old college coach at Henderson State. Don Dyer was now coaching at Central Arkansas University in Conway, a town in the central part of the state, north of Little Rock, the state capital.

Coach Wayne didn't make Scottie into something he wasn't. He didn't promise his former coach that he would be getting a star player. He truthfully told Coach Dyer that Scottie was an adequate point guard. He then added that there were some taller kids in the Pippen family and that Scottie might grow. He also suggested that Scottie would make a good manager under a work-study program. It wasn't the kind of referral a potential All-American would usually get.

Coach Dyer decided to give Scottie a chance. But he couldn't give him a basketball scholarship. Instead, Scottie would attend Central Arkansas with an educational grant to help pay his tuition. In return, he would serve as basketball team man-

Scottie Pippen started as an average basketball player who would have to work incredibly hard to prove that he could be a super-star. Here he poses for a picture in his high school yearbook as a senior.

ager. If he wanted to play, he'd have to prove he was good enough. "That's all I wanted," Scottie said. "A chance to go to college and a chance to compete."

Scottie arrived at the Conway campus in the fall of 1983 and surprised Coach Dyer. He had grown two inches and was now 6 feet 3 inches (190 centimeters). When basketball practice began, Scottie began his job of team manager, meeting the terms of his educational grant agreement. At the same time, he played as much pick-up basketball as he could, often going against members of the team. "It didn't take me long to realize I could be competitive with them," Scottie said.

Coach Dyer saw it, too. And when two players left the team shortly before the season began, Scottie suddenly found himself wearing a uniform. It was an exciting turnabout. He didn't play much his freshman year, however—he got into just 20 games for the Central Arkansas Bears. He averaged only 4.3 points a game and grabbed 59 rebounds.

Central Arkansas played against other small schools, most of which had second-rate talent. The best players were at the larger Division I schools. In fact, the Bears were an NAIA (National Association of Intercollegiate Athletics) school and not even part of the NCAA. Because of this, there was no way they could compete against the top schools

and better players. In addition, no player from an NAIA school had ever gone on to play in the NBA. A marginal point guard averaging 4.3 points a game would seem to have a limited future at best.

But Scottie didn't complain. He was playing college basketball and would have the opportunity to improve. When he returned for his sophomore year in the fall of 1984, he had grown again. Now he was 6 feet 5 inches (195 centimeters) and weighed 165 pounds (75 kilograms). He had played all summer back home and looked forward to the upcoming season.

If Scottie had been reading the papers, he'd have seen that the 1984 College Basketball Player of the Year, Michael Jordan, was now a rookie sensation with the Chicago Bulls. It's doubtful that Scottie even dreamed at that time of someday being a teammate of the NBA's newest phenom.

His job was to concentrate on his own game. Though still thin, Scottie had very long arms and huge hands. He also jumped very well. That enabled him to "play taller" than his height, and he began to show his improvement right from the beginning of the season. In 19 games his sophomore year, Scottie averaged 18.5 points, hitting an impressive 56.4 percent of his shots. He also snared 175 rebounds for an average of 9.2 a game. There was no doubt that he was now a ballplayer.

The overriding question was whether Scottie would get a chance at the NBA. There was no way he would ever be on the national stage at Central Arkansas, not when the Bears played against schools like Ouachita Baptist, the University of the Ozarks, and other tiny schools in Arkansas. Scottie wasn't being challenged by too many outstanding players. If he made it, he would have to do it on the merit of his own blossoming talent.

Some suggested that Scottie consider transferring to a bigger school. Even though that move would force him to sit out a year, he would be able to showcase his talents against the best in the nation. But it was Central Arkansas and Don Dyer who had given Scottie his chance, and at Central Arkansas he would stay. As a junior in 1985–1986 he had grown to 6 feet 6 inches (198 centimeters) and 185 pounds (84 kilograms). Now he was finally looking like a ballplayer.

That year, Scottie averaged 19.8 points in 29 games and began impressing those who saw him play. One of his biggest admirers was the assistant coach, Arch Jones, who was surprised how Scottie kept his game together even during a period of rapid physical growth. "He was able to take the skills he had learned when he was smaller and use them when he was bigger," Jones explained. "His arms are so long, his hands so big,

that he really plays like someone 6 feet 10 or 6 feet 11."

Scottie prepared for his senior year of 1986–1987 not knowing what the future would hold. He still wanted to play in the NBA, but he wasn't sure if he would get a chance to prove his worth, or whether he could even make it if given that chance. If this was going to be his final year of basketball, he decided that he would simply make the most of it and then return to Hamburg. "I knew some guys back home . . . and they would help me find some kind of job," he said. "I didn't know what, exactly. But I knew they would come up with something for me."

That season Scottie began playing the best basketball of his life. Now at his full height of 6 feet 7 inches (200 centimeters), he had become a dominant player. But was it the small-school competition that made him dominant? Or could he have the same success against better competition?

Scottie was averaging nearly 24 points a game as a senior, grabbing 10 rebounds, and hitting nearly 60 percent of his shots. Unfortunately, the rest of the players weren't close to his caliber and the team wouldn't get a chance to go to the NAIA tournament in Kansas City, Missouri. But what Scottie didn't know was that the word about his talent was starting to get out. During a routine game that

February, a man named Marty Blake was in the stands.

Blake was the head of NBA scouting, and after watching Scottie he called Jerry Krause, the general manager of the Chicago Bulls. Blake told Krause that there was a kid at tiny Central Arkansas who might be worth a further look. Krause made a note of it. Scottie finished the season with a 23.6 average, 10 rebounds, and a 59.2 shooting percentage.

When Scottie went to Portsmouth, Virginia, to play in a postseason amateur tournament, Jerry Krause saw him play for the first time. The Bulls' GM was impressed right away. "The players came out for warm-ups, hadn't even shot the ball," Krause remembered. "Here's this guy. He's got the longest arms I've ever seen. I've always been very big on long arms and big hands. I thought to myself, 'There's something special.' And when I looked around, everybody else was murmuring, too."

Finally, college basketball's best-kept secret was coming out. From there, Scottie was invited to a number of pre-draft tryout camps. At these, he would finally be competing against some of the best collegians in the country. Arch Jones accompanied Scottie to one of the tryout camps in Chicago. Even the assistant coach was awed. "I never realized how good he really was until I saw him with all the other players at the tryout camp," Jones said. "Scottie

When Bulls general manager
Jerry Krause first observed
Scottie's play, Krause was
impressed and said that Scottie
had "the longest arms [he'd]
ever seen." Those long arms
have served Scottie well, as they
do in this action against the New
Jersey Nets.

made a move where he came in from the right and banked the ball off the backboard with his left hand. And when he'd go up the middle . . . dunk city."

The more Scottie played, the more heads turned. Everyone wanted to know where this thin kid with the never-changing facial expression had come from. His skill level was extremely high. He had great jumping ability and solid basketball instincts. Only Scottie knew the dues he had paid to reach this point. "Nobody knows how hard I worked alone on dribbling and just feeling the ball in my hands," he said.

By the end of the tryout camps Scottie had emerged. Suddenly, a number of NBA general managers were buzzing about the kid from Hamburg being a real prize.

Krause had originally thought he might try to grab Scottie on the second round of the 1987 draft. Now, he began to question whether Scottie would still be available by the second round. The Bulls, in fact, had the eighth pick in the first round. Krause was worried whether Scottie Pippen would last even *that* long.

From tiny Central Arkansas to a place among the top seven players in the land, Scottie had made a huge leap. Not wanting to lose a chance to draft Scottie, Krause struck a deal with the Seattle SuperSonics. To this day, it stands as one of the most brilliant moves in NBA history.

The Sonics had the fifth pick in the first round. With that pick, they drafted Scottie. The Bulls then used their eighth pick to take 7-foot (213-centimeter) center, Olden Polynice. According to the pre-arranged deal, the two teams traded draft picks. Scottie Pippen was now the property of the Chicago Bulls. "This is a dream come true," Scottie said, "something I never imagined would happen, not in a million years."

When he came to his first NBA training camp in the fall of 1987, Scottie would be meeting his new teammates, including the Bulls' resident superstar, Michael Jordan.

3 THE JORDAN LEGEND BEGINS

Though it's hard to believe, Michael Jordan was not the top draft choice of the NBA in 1984. The Houston Rockets had the first pick that year and chose Akeem (now Hakeem) Olajuwon, an All-American center from the University of Houston. That was no surprise. Olajuwon was considered a potential dominant center, exactly what he turned out to be. The Portland Trail Blazers had the next pick, and everyone figured that they'd jump for Jordan.

But the Blazers tabbed 7-foot-1-inch (216-centimeter) center Sam Bowie of Kentucky, who turned out to be an average, injury-prone player. The third pick that year belonged to the Chicago Bulls. When

the Bulls heard that the Blazers had gone for Bowie, they couldn't contain themselves. Without waiting for a moment to pass, they grabbed Michael. That made him the third overall pick in the draft.

Michael was in Los Angeles at draft time, helping the United States Olympic basketball team win a gold medal. In fact, he was the team's leading scorer with a 17.1 average and had emerged as the squad's biggest star. It was a foreshadowing of things to come.

Before Michael arrived, the Bulls had been going through a down period. Bulls officials seemed to sense immediately that they had a player around whom to build for a more successful future. Michael's first contract was for $6.15 million over seven years. He would turn out to be worth every single penny.

It became apparent that the pros would see a different Michael Jordan from the one who played at North Carolina. At Carolina, Michael stayed within Coach Dean Smith's system and learned. There was little opportunity for him to step out and shine as an individual player. But the Bulls' coach, Kevin Loughery, saw no reason to restrain Michael. He told Michael to go out there and do his thing.

Within weeks of the season's start, it was apparent that the NBA had a new star. Michael was showing an incredible array of skills. He was blow-

ing past, jumping over, and spinning around veteran players, who just couldn't stop him. In his third game, he exploded for 37 points against the Milwaukee Bucks. Two weeks later, in his ninth professional game, he erupted for 45 in a victory over the San Antonio Spurs.

In a short time he had taken his place alongside the game's two resident superstars, Magic Johnson of the Los Angeles Lakers and Larry Bird of the Boston Celtics. They were the players everyone wanted to see. Now reporters in each city were asking about Michael's amazing drives and dunks. They couldn't believe how he would seemingly hang in the air making two or three moves while defenders fell by the wayside. He hadn't done much of that at North Carolina. "I never practice the fancy stuff," Michael said. "If I thought about a move, I'd probably make a turnover. I just look at a situation in the air, adjust, create, and let instinct take over."

By midseason, Michael was one of the most sought after, charismatic athletes in the country. As Phoenix Suns marketing director Harvey Shank said, "Michael Jordan is already in a class by himself. It's the way he gives himself to the game and his God-given talents. Michael Jordan coming to town is like a major entertainer appearing in Phoenix. People line up outside his locker room before warmups just to get a glimpse of him."

Just midway through his rookie season, Michael was already poised for super-stardom. He was a charismatic and sought-after athlete from the very beginning. Here he sports his famous "Air Jordan" basketball shoes.

Michael finished his rookie season with a 28.2 scoring average. His 2,313 points were the third-highest in the league. But Michael did more than score. He led the team in rebounding with 6.5 per game, in assists with 481, and in steals with 196. Better yet, the Bulls made the playoffs with a 38–44 record. Though they lost to Milwaukee in four games, it was still a step in the right direction.

Not surprisingly, at season's end Michael was named the NBA's Rookie of the Year. And by that time, he was already being sought after to endorse products. His Air Jordan basketball shoe, manufactured by Nike, was a runaway best-seller. It had been a difficult decision for him to leave Carolina a year early. But now he knew that it had been the right choice.

The beginning of the 1985–1986 basketball season provided an interesting contrast for the future teammates. In Conway, Arkansas, Scottie Pippen was about to begin his junior year at Central Arkansas. No one outside of Conway knew what kind of ballplayer he was, and most in Conway never thought he would be in the NBA.

At the same time, people all around the National Basketball Association couldn't wait to see Michael Jordan perform for the Bulls. If his rookie year was any indication, Michael was really going to be something to see this year. When he scored

35 points in the opener against the Cleveland Cavaliers and 33 in the Bulls' next game with the Detroit Pistons, he looked better than ever.

But in game three it all came crashing down for Michael. Playing against the Golden State Warriors, Michael flew in for one of his spectacular slam dunks. After completing the jam, Michael landed flat-footed, instead of his usual toe-to-heel landing. He felt the pain in his left foot immediately. The medical diagnosis wasn't good—Michael had broken the tarsal navicular bone in his left foot.

Doctors said that Michael would be out at least six weeks. It was apparent how much the Bulls missed him when they lost eight of their next nine games. But for Michael, the agony was not being able to play. "I've never really gone through anything like this and I don't really know how to deal with it," he said.

Michael spent time at his new home in Northbrook, Illinois, and then went back to Chapel Hill, where he saw old friends and continued to study for his college degree in geography. "In the beginning [after the injury], the days were going so slow that I found myself just sitting around, counting the minutes," Michael said. "Then I realized that I had to put my mind to work, keep myself occupied."

By Christmas, when Michael was supposed to return to the lineup, an examination showed that the bone still had not healed enough. The permanent cast he'd been wearing was replaced by a lighter walking cast. February 1 was set as his target date to play again. A late January X ray, however, showed that there were still signs of the fracture. The team didn't want to take a chance with a player of Michael's value. They said that he couldn't play until doctors said the bone was fully healed.

Michael returned to Chapel Hill. He was disappointed because he had such a strong desire to play—and before long that desire got the best of him. He began to work out against doctors' orders. No one outside of Chapel Hill knew what he was doing.

"I started gradually," he said. "First I just took free throws, then began moving around and taking shots. Finally, we got up a couple of two-on-two games, slow motion, then three-on-three. One day some of the guys began playing five-on-five, full court, and I just got involved."

Michael said that the toughest part was mental. He continued to question whether he should be playing. But he also sensed his game returning and that felt good. Then came the final barrier. "When I finally dunked, it just felt wonderful," he said.

Michael told the Bulls and the doctors what he had done. They weren't pleased with the news at first. Doctors felt that there was still a small chance he would reinjure the foot by playing. The team considered making him sit out until the following season. "If I had to sit out the rest of the year, I would go crazy," Michael said. "I feel I want to test the foot now."

The team finally relented and Michael returned on March 15. Without him in the lineup, the Bulls had slipped to 21—43. So when he took the court against the Milwaukee Bucks, excitement was high. Everyone was nervous. Michael played just 14 minutes and scored 12 points. But the highlight of his return was a skyward slam dunk over 7-foot-3-inch (220-centimeter) Randy Breuer. After landing, Michael sprinted down court without a limp. The foot had passed its first test.

Michael's minutes increased as the season wound down. In the next to last game of the year, he scored 31 points as the Bulls topped the Washington Bullets 105–103 to clinch a playoff spot. Michael had averaged 22.7 points in just 18 games in the regular season. Ever the showman, he was about to remind the entire NBA just what he was made of.

The Bulls, with the poorest record of all 16 playoff teams, had to face Larry Bird and the pow-

erful Boston Celtics in the first round in a best-of-five series. In the first game, Michael dominated Bird, Kevin McHale, and Robert Parish, the Celtics stars. He soared over them, blew past them, and twisted and turned his way to the basket. Boston defenders couldn't stop him. When it ended, he had scored 49 points, even though the Bulls lost. Not only did Michael want to win, he felt he had something to prove. "I want to win very badly," he said, after the game. "My whole season is wrapped up in these playoffs. I want to do the things I couldn't do all season. When you're out of sight, people tend to forget you. I'm a competitor and I like to be respected as a player."

But no one was about to forget Michael Jordan. In game two at the Boston Garden he was even more unstoppable. The Bulls kept isolating Michael on one side, giving him room to operate, and the Celtics couldn't stop him. After his long layoff, he seemed to be enjoying every moment of the action. When he hit two free throws at the end of regulation time the score was tied at 116–116. Michael had scored 54 of the Bulls' points!

The game would eventually go into double overtime with the Celtics pulling it out, 135–131. But the buzz all around the NBA was about Michael Jordan. He had played 53 minutes, hit 22 of 41 shots from the floor, and 19 of 21 from the free

Although the Celtics eliminated the Bulls in the first round of the 1986 playoffs, Michael gave an outstanding performance that caused the legendary Larry Bird (number 33) to claim that Michael was God in disguise.

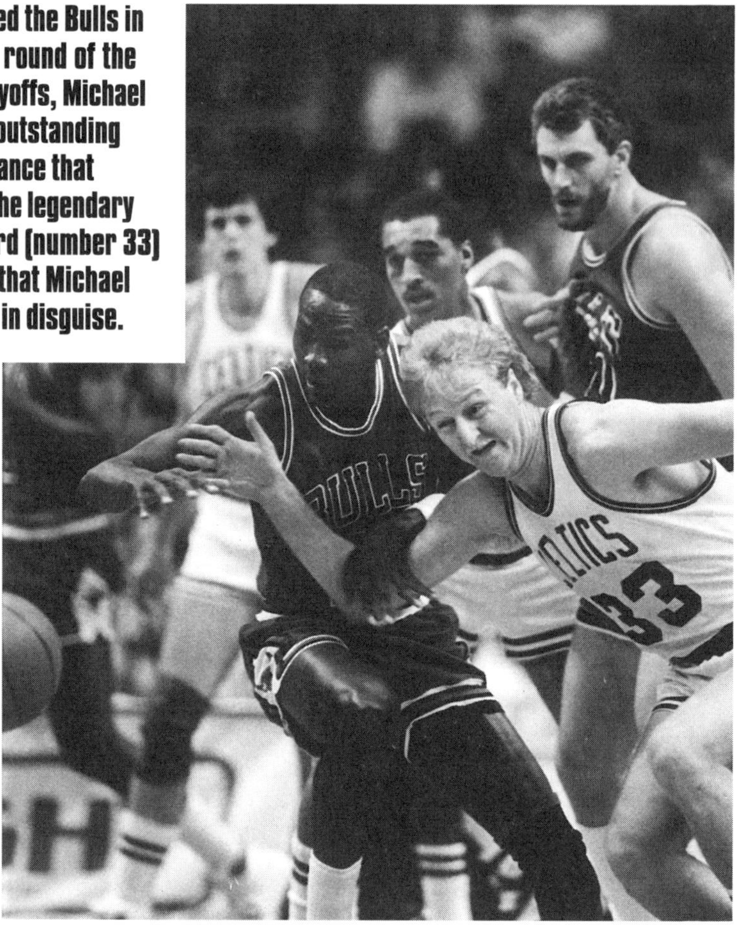

throw line for an incredible 63 points. "As you can see, no one can guard him," said the Celtics' Dennis Johnson, one of the best defensive players in the league. And the legendary Larry Bird said that the player who had scored 63 points against his team was "God disguised as Michael Jordan."

Even though the Celtics closed the Bulls out in three straight games, Michael had produced an incredible series. He averaged 43.7 points for the three games and sounded a warning to the basketball world. He was healthy again and ready to play.

As Scottie Pippen began his senior year of 1986–1987 at Central Arkansas trying to prove to others and himself that he had a shot at the NBA, Michael Jordan was about to show everyone that he might just be the greatest individual talent in basketball history. The Bulls had a new coach in Doug Collins, but the overall talent was still thin. The only other player of All-Star caliber besides Michael was power forward Charles Oakley.

The Bulls opened the season against the Knicks at Madison Square Garden in New York. Midway through the fourth period the Knicks had a 90–85 lead with the momentum of the game swinging their way. Collins called a time-out, but before he could outline his strategy, Michael interrupted him. "Don't worry, coach," Michael said. "I'm not going to let you lose your first game."

Michael then went out and played like a man possessed. He went around, past, and over the be-wildered Knicks. When the smoke cleared, the Bulls had a 108–103 victory. Michael had scored 21 fourth-quarter points en route to a 50-point perfor-mance. The season had officially begun.

From there, Michael went on a real tear. He scored 40 or more points in 13 of his next 16 games,

including nine in a row. Yet in spite of his efforts, the Bulls were just about at the .500 mark (they had only won as many games as they lost). He couldn't make the team a winner by himself, but he continued to try nonetheless. In one game against the Knicks, he scored 18-straight Bulls' points, an NBA record. And later in the year, against Sacramento, he broke his own record with a run of 23 straight in a 61-point night.

When the season ended, the Bulls had just a 40–42 record, but made the playoffs again. Michael had won his first NBA scoring crown with a 37.1 average. In doing so, he became the only NBA player besides Wilt Chamberlain to score more than 3,000 points in a season. He was also the first NBA player ever to have more than 200 steals (236) and 100 blocked shots (125) in the same year. It had truly been a remarkable season.

In the off-season, Michael kept a promise to his parents and returned to North Carolina to complete his degree in geography. By this time, he was a full-fledged celebrity who couldn't go out in public without being surrounded by enthusiastic fans. Bulls General Manager Jerry Krause said he had almost become a "cult" figure. Even Coach Collins said Michael had to live something of a lonely life. "There's a time when you like to sit down in a movie with four or five of your buddies, eat some

popcorn, laugh, and have a good time," the coach said. "That's taken away from you when you're as popular as Michael."

But Michael was prepared to deal with all that. He remained one of the most courteous athletes anywhere when dealing with the media and began to endorse more products as a public spokesman. But above all, he wanted the Chicago Bulls to become a championship team. To achieve that, he knew he needed help.

Having acquired Scottie Pippen in the first round of the 1987 NBA draft, the Bulls used their next pick to acquire 6-foot-10-inch (208-centimeter) power forward Horace Grant of Clemson. Veterans Oakley, Corzine, and guard John Paxson were also back. Hopefully, everyone would mesh to make the Bulls a winner.

Scottie was the unknown quantity. His physical skills were obvious, but it wasn't easy for an NAIA or other small-school player to come into the NBA. He was the first NAIA player ever to be drafted. And being a first-rounder only added to the pressure he had to face.

General Manager Krause knew he had taken a big chance. A team getting the fifth player chosen

in the draft should come away with a major talent. "If Scottie didn't become the player I thought he could be, he'd have gone down as Krause's folly," the GM said. "I'd have been ripped from pillar to post."

As soon as training camp opened, Scottie showed that he was there to work, and he knew that he had a very special teacher to learn from firsthand. Scottie insisted that he guard Michael Jordan at every practice—if he was going to be taken to school, he would learn from the best. "I figured he couldn't do anything to me that he hadn't already done to somebody else," was the way Scottie put it.

Day after day, the two went head-to-head in practice. Michael, being so competitive, didn't let up at all on the rookie, and showed him his entire array of moves, drives, and shots. Scottie had never played against anyone of this caliber before, so he struggled at times, but also showed his great athleticism.

The Bulls surprised everyone that year, getting off to a fast start. They won seven of their first eight games, and 12 of their first 15. Michael, of course, was as sensational as ever, often carrying the team on his back and almost always producing at crunch time, when the game was on the line. And he began getting more help from the other players.

Neither Scottie nor Horace Grant were stars from the first. Both rookies were worked into the lineup gradually, contributing in spurts and learning about the rigors of NBA play. While each was helping the team, there was still no real indication of how good either would eventually become. But the Bulls as a team had certainly become better.

They finished the season with a 50–32 record, winning 18 of their final 25 games after a midseason slump. This time Michael led the league with 2,868 points and a 35.0 average in 82 games. He was over the 40-point mark 16 times, and scored more than 50 on four occasions. He also led the league in steals with 259 and had 131 blocked shots. That was more blocks than 16 starting centers had. "People see me as just a scorer," he said, "somebody who shoots a lot and doesn't do much else. So this year I was determined to show my all-around game."

That he did. He was a first team All-Star, a member of the All-Defensive first team. He then became the first player ever to be named Defensive Player of the Year and the league's Most Valuable Player in the same year. Michael was doing it all. After just four seasons in the league, he was already being called the greatest ever.

But it was winning the MVP Award that really made Michael proud. "It's a thrill, and I'm really

happy," he said. "Winning this award has always been one of my biggest goals in basketball."

Scottie, however, didn't make the same kind of sensational debut Michael had made as a rookie. He needed experience, and Coach Collins worked him into the lineup slowly. Scottie averaged about 21 minutes a game, scoring at a 7.9 clip, grabbing 298 rebounds, with 91 steals, and 52 blocked shots. He also had 169 assists. At this early stage, he was showing flashes of an all-around game.

In the playoffs, the Bulls won their first round series against the Cleveland Cavaliers, then were beaten by the tough Detroit Pistons in five games, 4–1. Michael averaged 36.3 points in 10 playoff games, while Scottie raised the level of his game and averaged 10 points a game in the playoffs.

Scottie was pleased with the way his rookie year turned out. The thing that gave him the most pleasure, however, was that he was able to send his father a videotape of his first pro game. Preston Pippen couldn't travel because of the stroke he had suffered, and the tape was the only way he could see his son play. "The stroke took away my father's ability to speak," Scottie said. "But my mom told me that when he watched the tape he cried."

Now that Scottie had made it to the NBA, he focused on elevating his game. Playing alongside

Michael, and going up against him in practice, showed Scottie the kind of ballplayer he wanted to be—a player who excelled at every phase of the game and at both ends of the court.

There was one setback to endure. During the off-season Scottie underwent back surgery to correct an old problem and missed the entire preseason as well as the first eight games of the 1988 season. But by that time, the Bulls had made some trades. They sent Charles Oakley to the Knicks in return for 7-foot-1-inch (216-centimeter) center Bill Cartwright. That move allowed Horace Grant to take over at power forward. The club also drafted 7-foot (213-centimeter) center Will Perdue as a backup and acquired veteran guard Craig Hodges, a good long-range shooter.

With all the new players, the team got off to a slow start. Scottie rejoined the club in the ninth game. And as soon as he got himself into game shape, he moved in as the starting small forward. He had come an incredibly long way in a short time. In five years, he had gone from team manager at a tiny school in Arkansas to starting forward for the Chicago Bulls. He sure didn't want to blow it now.

The team continued to play better as the season progressed, finishing with a 47–35 record. Michael once again led the league in scoring with

When this picture was taken during the 1988-1989 season, the Bulls were still putting together a championship team. Although no one knew it at the time, the two main elements of this team were already sharing the court. Michael wears number 23, and Scottie wears number 33.

a 32.5 average. He also had his best rebounding year, averaging 8 per game. Scottie's peer Horace Grant also showed improvement, averaging 12 points a game and leading the club in rebounds with 681 for the season.

But perhaps the biggest improvement was made by Scottie himself. He was second to Michael in scoring with a 14.4 average in 73 games. He had 445 rebounds and was second to Jordan in steals, as well, with 139. Many still considered the Bulls a one-man team—Jordan and his supporting cast. In fact, there were even times when Michael used that term to describe his teammates. There certainly was some truth to it. Michael was the superstar. None of the other players had shown themselves to be All-Star caliber.

It was in the playoffs in 1989 that the Bulls really proved they were close to being one of the elite teams in the NBA. First they whipped the Cavaliers in five games. Next they took the New York Knicks in six. Now they would meet the Pistons in the conference finals. The winner of the best-of-seven series would play for the championship.

The series was hard-fought from the first. The Pistons, led by Isiah Thomas, Dennis Rodman, and Bill Laimbeer, were known as the NBA's bad boys, but the Bulls held their own. They won two of the first three in Chicago, but back in Detroit the Pis-

tons prevailed. They had a 3–2 lead going into game six. In the first few minutes of the game, Scottie took a hard elbow from center Laimbeer and was knocked unconscious. He was taken to the bench and didn't return to the game. The Bulls were beaten and many doubted Scottie's toughness when he did not reenter the game.

Jerry Krause was quick to defend him. "[Scottie] is a tougher kid than most people think," the GM said. "He begged me to let him go back into that game. He just begged me and begged me. But in the end, I had to go with the doctor's advice."

The season ended on a sour note. Michael still hadn't won his championship and Scottie had to prove something more than that. It was something they would have to do as teammates. It wouldn't work any other way.

5 GOING TO THE TOP

Prior to the 1989–1990 season the Bulls continued to fine-tune their machine, adding a few more pieces to the puzzle. Two prominent rookies were forward/center Stacey King and guard B. J. Armstrong. The Bulls felt that if Scottie continued to improve, he would eventually become a second superstar, the player they needed to complement Michael.

The Bulls also made a coaching change, elevating Phil Jackson from assistant coach to the top spot. Jackson was a former NBA player who had coached in the Continental League before coming to the Bulls. He was also a man who related very well to the modern-day athlete. Jackson felt that this was a team that could win.

Jackson was right, but it would take some time. The team was good, but not quite good enough. The Bulls finished the year at 55–27, just four games behind the defending champion Pistons in the Central Division. Michael won his fourth straight scoring title, averaging 33.6 points a game and also leading the league with 227 steals. He was as spectacular as usual, from his 54-point effort in the opening game to his career-best 69 points in a win over Cleveland on March 28.

In his third season, Scottie had shown tremendous improvement. He was an All-Star selection for the first time, participating in the mid-season All-Star Game. His scoring average was up to 16.5 points. He was third in the league in steals with 211 and grabbed 547 rebounds, just 18 fewer than Michael. He also led the Bulls with 101 blocked shots, and had 444 assists, an impressive number for a forward. It was also a year in which he built a new home for his parents in Arkansas. That gave him as much satisfaction as his biggest games on the hardwood.

The Bulls looked as if they meant business when the playoffs began. First, they polished off the Bucks in four games. Next came the Philadelphia 76ers with their superstar forward Charles Barkley. And, like so many times in the past, the series turned into the Michael Jordan show. Michael

had 39 and 45 points in the first two games, each of which the Bulls won. When the 76ers took the third game, it was despite Michael's 49 points.

The Bulls won the fourth game 111–101. Michael had scored 18 in the final period to put it on ice. He finished with 45 points, 11 assists, 6 rebounds, 2 steals, and 2 blocks. It was a completely dominating, incredible performance.

Michael could do it all, and he could do it better than anyone. The Bulls then closed out the Sixers in five games and prepared for a rematch with the defending champion Pistons. The Detroit game plan was geared to stopping Michael. Scottie was not yet considered a threat. He was good, but he still wasn't dominant. Would he finally earn some real respect against the champs?

At first, the Pistons made it look easy. They won the first two games in Detroit. Then Michael did something he had never done before. He chewed out his teammates. He gave them a message in no uncertain terms. "He said the guys were playing lousy ball," admitted forward Horace Grant. "He didn't want to name names, but he was right. The guys know who they were. We were embarrassed. Mike feels the guys aren't giving their all, and I don't blame him . . . We played terribly. I've never seen Michael that upset."

Scottie also got the message. "What Michael did was a wake-up call for us," he said. Perhaps no

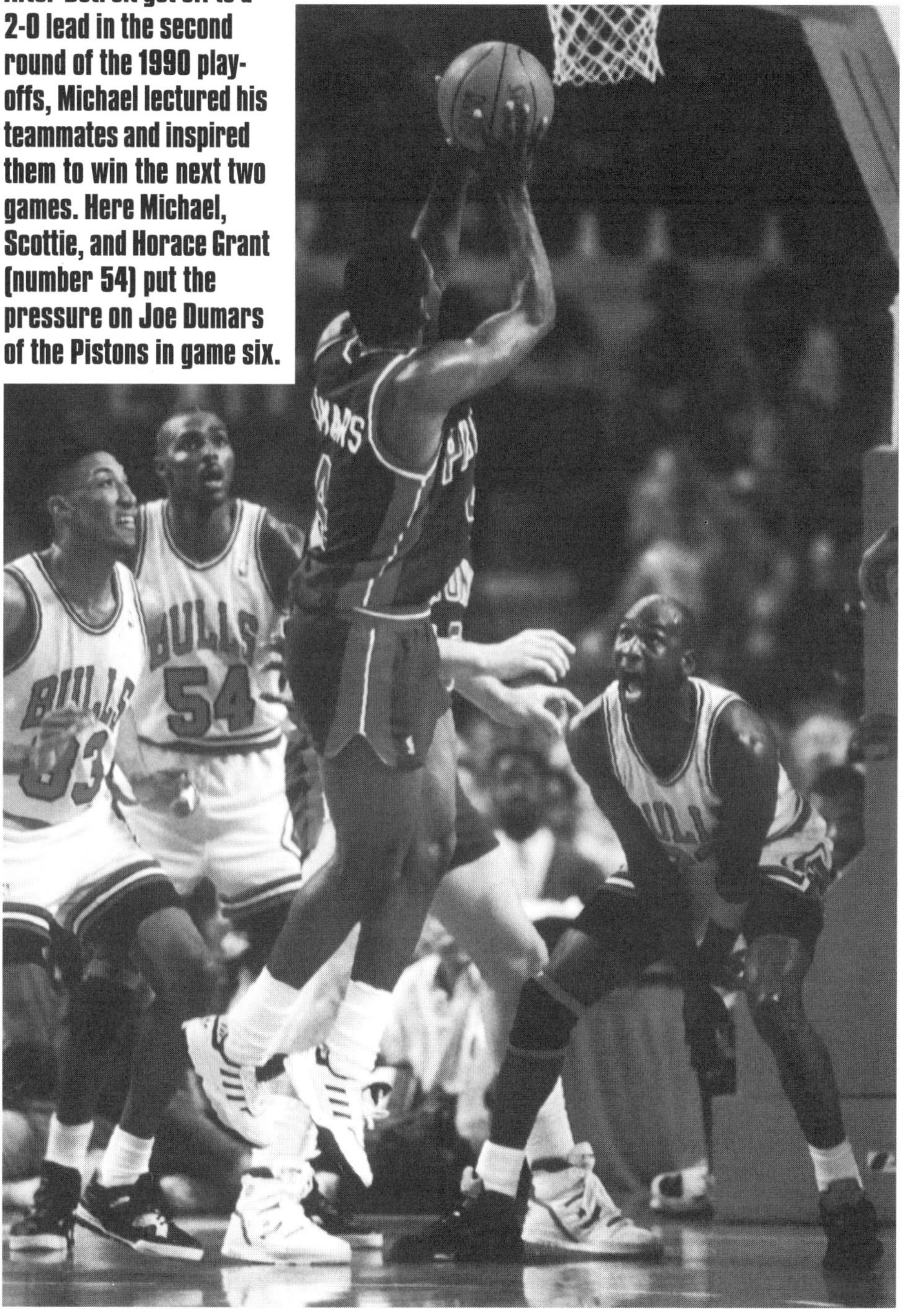

After Detroit got off to a
2-0 lead in the second
round of the 1990 play-
offs, Michael lectured his
teammates and inspired
them to win the next two
games. Here Michael,
Scottie, and Horace Grant
(number 54) put the
pressure on Joe Dumars
of the Pistons in game six.

one took Michael's words to heart as Scottie did. He was already playing with a personal burden. During the conference semifinal series with Philadelphia, his father had died back home in Hamburg. It had been a challenge to stay focused on basketball.

Michael's speech seemed to work. In the third game back in Chicago, the Bulls turned it up several notches. Michael exploded as only he could do, scoring 47 points, including 31 in the second half and 18 in the fourth quarter. But in this game he had more help from Scottie, who chipped in with 29 points as the Bulls won, 107–102. The two had scored 76 of the team's 107 points. For one of the first times in a big game they showed just what a devastating pair of teammates they could be. And, of course, they both played well on the defensive end of the floor.

After that, the series became a dogfight. The Bulls won the fourth game. The teams then split the next two, setting up a seventh and deciding game. Once again, Chicago was a win away from playing for the championship. Scottie was having a breakthrough series. Through six games he was complementing Michael beautifully, averaging 19 points and 6.7 rebounds—very close to a superstar performance.

But as game seven in Detroit got under way, Scottie seemed oddly out of sync. He was missing

his shots and not being aggressive under the boards. After hitting just one of 10 shots, he came to the bench. As the Pistons began opening a large lead, Scottie remained on the bench, an ice pack on his head. It wasn't until after the Pistons' 93–74 victory that the fans found out what had happened. Scottie had come down with a severe migraine headache. He had tried to play, but was totally ineffective.

Once again critics claimed that Scottie always looked for an excuse at crunch time, that he really lacked the guts to compete in big games. They cited the elbow he had taken from Laimbeer the season before. Two years in a row he had been on the bench during the team's biggest game of the year.

"I'd never had a migraine before," Scottie said, afterward. "Migraine headaches happen to people all the time. It just happened to me at the wrong time. People want results, not excuses. If I had been able to play up to my ability, I think we would have won. I know [that] when I'm at full strength, I am one of the best players in the game."

Scottie had real confidence in his ability. It was the headache that had knocked him out of the box. "It was like someone had put an ice pick in my head," he admitted. "I was afraid I was dying."

Scottie went to the hospital a short time later and had a brain scan, just to make sure that he was all right. He also sought out the advice of

former NBA stars such as Julius Erving and Kareem Abdul-Jabbar. Abdul-Jabbar had also suffered from recurring migraines throughout his great career. After listening to advice from these sources he decided to make some changes in his lifestyle that would better prepare him for the long season.

"Now I eat a good breakfast, then don't eat again until after the game," he said later. "I also make sure I get my sleep. I always take a nap in the afternoon on the day of a game. I lie in bed, visualize the game, think about who I am guarding and the things he likes to do. It all helps."

Despite scoring only two points in the final game with the Pistons, Scottie still averaged 19.3 points in 15 playoff games. He seemed poised to make a major breakthrough in 1990–1991. And so did the rest of the Bulls.

Early in the new season, however, Scottie wasn't shooting well. That's when Coach Jackson suggested he relax, not worry about his shooting, and play his all-around game. In the team's next outing against the L.A. Clippers, Scottie posted a triple double, scoring 13 points, grabbing 13 rebounds, and handing out 12 assists. Coach Jackson called the game a turning point. "I think Scottie realized that even though he had barely scored in double figures [in the game], there were plenty of other ways he could help this team win besides just scoring points."

In 1990–1991, the Bulls were winning big. Michael was in his usual spot atop the league's scorers, though his average was down a couple of points. But that was because the other players were contributing more. Horace Grant had become a fine power forward. The veteran Bill Cartwright lent his experience and skill at center. John Paxson and B. J. Armstrong combined to do a fine job at point guard, while Will Perdue was giving the team solid minutes behind Cartwright.

But perhaps the biggest change in the Bulls that year was Scottie Pippen's conversion from player to star to superstar. Those in the NBA saw it long before the fans. It was revealed in the little things like his overall play at both ends of the court. In his fourth year in the league, Scottie was finally becoming the teammate Michael needed, and the two players now led the Bulls toward the top. "Scottie is a transformed player," said Washington Bullets forward Bernard King. "He's one of the few guys who's a complete player in the NBA."

Scottie gave much of the credit to Coach Jackson for allowing him to begin reaching his potential. "I think when Phil took over everyone found it easier to accept their roles because they had the freedom to try contributing a little more," Scottie said. "It's a delicate thing to . . . come in as a top draft pick, to want to be treated as a top-caliber player in the league and find yourself constantly

overshadowed by someone like Michael. But the only way we could have gotten better was to let us go out and play and see what else we've got. If we'd kept being held back, we'd have never known."

The Bulls ended the season with a 61–21 record. It was the best in franchise history and gave them the Central Division title by 11 games over the defending champion Pistons.

Scottie upped his scoring average to 17.8. He also had career bests in rebounds (595) and assists (511). For the first time he topped Michael in both those categories, showing his increased responsibilities with the team. In fact, he led the Bulls in assists, something extremely unusual for a player operating at forward.

Michael won his fifth-straight scoring crown with a 31.5 average, and also won his second Most Valuable Player award. "This is well received by myself, my family, and my teammates," he said. "Most of the credit, though, should go to my teammates, who have stepped up and put us in this position. When a team wins, all the individual accolades follow."

In the playoffs, the Bulls proved that their success had not been a fluke. First, they whipped the New York Knicks in three straight games. Next, they toppled the 76ers in five games, 4–1. And when

they met the Pistons for the conference title, it was sweet revenge. The aging bad boys of Detroit were no match for the multilevel talents of the Bulls, now led by Jordan and Pippen.

No one predicted that it would be this easy. But the Bulls, humming along like a well-oiled machine, blew out the Pistons in four straight games. The fourth and final game seemed to symbolize what the Bulls had become—they won it comfortably, 115–94. Michael led the way with 29 points, and Scottie was right behind him with 23. Grant had 16 and John Paxson scored 12. "I've got to give so much credit to Scottie Pippen, Horace Grant, and the rest of the supporting cast," Michael said afterward. "This is a big step for the city and the fans. Now we go to the finals, and we'll do our best to win it."

In the finals, the Bulls met the Los Angeles Lakers. The Lakers, led by Magic Johnson, had won five NBA titles in the 1980s. But, like the Pistons, they were an aging team. Superstar center Kareem Abdul-Jabbar had retired after the 1989 season, but the Lakers still had some solid talent behind Magic. They proved it in the opening game when a three-pointer by Sam Perkins in the final seconds keyed a 93–91 Lakers upset in the opener in Chicago.

In game two, however, the Bulls turned it around. Michael torched the Lakers for 33 points,

while Scottie and Horace Grant scored 20 each, and John Paxson added 16 in a 107–86 victory. Scottie did more than score, however. Coach Jackson had him guard the 6-foot-9-inch (205-centimeter) Johnson, and Scottie was brilliant. He held Magic to just 14 points on 4-for-13 shooting from the floor. There was little doubt now that he was becoming a star at both ends of the floor.

From there, the Bulls went on to take the next three games and win their first championship. The fifth and final game gave yet another indication that Scottie Pippen had raised his play to sit alongside Michael Jordan as one of the premier stars in the NBA. In Chicago's 108–101 victory, Michael and Scottie both played the entire 48 minutes. Scottie had 32 points; Michael had 30. The two of them were also demons on defense, compiling 10 steals between them. They were both all over the court.

Michael had averaged 31.1 points in 17 play-off games. He had 108 rebounds, 142 assists, 40 steals, and 23 blocks. Scottie averaged 21.6 points, had 151 rebounds, 99 assists, 42 steals, and 19 blocked shots. Both players had been outstanding, a one-two punch with the ability to control the outcome of a game.

The championship was especially emotional for Michael. He had been with the Bulls for seven years and had been through the tough times be-

fore the team was a winner. "This means so much to the team and the city of Chicago," he said. "It was a seven-year struggle. We started from scratch, at the bottom. But every year we worked harder and harder, until we got it. . . . And we did it as a team all season long."

As for Scottie, he felt the title was vindication for those who still pointed to the games he had left against Detroit the previous two seasons. He would prove his worth even more over the next two years, with two more championships for the Bulls. In 1992, the team was 67–15 in the regular season and topped the Portland Trail Blazers in six games for the title. The following year they compiled a 57–25 mark to win another division title, and then defeated the Phoenix Suns in six games to win a third-straight championship.

During that time, Michael continued to solidify his reputation. He won another pair of scoring titles with averages of 30.1 and 32.6 points per game. He had now been the league's top scorer seven straight times. He won his third MVP crown after the 1991–1992 season, was a first team All-NBA selection every year, as well as a selection on the All-Defensive Team.

Accolades for Michael came from every corner of the basketball community. Former coach and TV commentator Jack Ramsay called him "the finest

athlete I've ever seen in the NBA. He's not only a great player, but a class individual as well."

Teammate John Paxson, a key role player for the Bulls, expressed his feelings about playing alongside Michael. "I accepted a long time ago that Michael is the greatest athlete in the sport, maybe in the world," Paxson said. "And you've got to accept your role. Michael's challenged me at times. The great ones do that."

As for Scottie, he was rapidly becoming a great one in his own right. His scoring average during the second and third title runs was 21 and 18.6 a game. He was over the 600 rebound mark in each season while continuing to lead the team in assists. In both 1992 and 1993 he made the All-Defensive first team and was on the All-NBA second and third teams. Many felt that he should be on the first team.

Bill Walton, a former star center who had become a broadcaster, already had Scottie close to the top. "You think about it," Walton said. "Scottie Pippen might just be the second-best all-around player in the league. Who's better, outside of Michael? Who does more things?"

Coach Jackson explained how Scottie's role had expanded to the point where Scottie had joined Michael to make a pair of multitalented, do-it-all teammates. "[Scottie's] role here has continued to

grow," the coach said. "As more and more teams pressed us [defensively], we decided we had to become more creative in our response. More and more we had to go to Michael to bring the ball up. We didn't want to do that. Then we came up with the thought of Scottie as a third ball advancer, of an offense that attacked at multiple points. From that position, he started being able to take control, to make decisions. He became a little bit of everything."

Off the court, the two players had different lifestyles. Michael was married with two children. Scottie was single. Michael was a complete celebrity, recognizable through his many TV commercials and public appearances. His time away from the game was always tight. Scottie was closer as a friend to Horace Grant at this point in his career. In fact, he actually seemed to prefer anonymity after seeing what Michael had to go through. "No, I wouldn't ever want to be him," Scottie said, when asked if he would like to change places with Michael. "To have to stay in the room all day long, because so many people are waiting outside? To always have the feeling that someone is standing behind you, listening, just recording everything you say and do? No. I don't know how he does it.

"I can go out. I can walk around. People come up to me for autographs and to talk, but it's natu-

After Michael and
Scottie had played
together for a few
seasons, it was easy to
see how their lives off
the court differed.
Michael was a super-
star who was married
and had children, while
Scottie was a bachelor
who could go out in
public and remain
anonymous. Here
Michael is pictured
with Jeffrey, one of his
sons, at a celebration
after the Bulls' first
championship in 1991.

ral. They see Michael and they jump. People act as if they've seen a ghost. I wouldn't want to live like that."

Although they weren't particularly close off the court, as teammates Michael and Scottie made beautiful music together. The team had won three straight titles. Many felt that they could win more, and maybe even approach the record of eight straight that had been set by the Boston Celtics years earlier. But after the 1993 season, something would happen that would change the lives and destinies of both superstar players.

6
SCOTTIE GOES IT ALONE

Everything seemed on target for a fourth-straight title. It was difficult to see any team dethroning the Bulls in 1994. But in July 1993, a news story broke that caught the attention of people across the nation. Michael Jordan's father, James, was missing. Mr. Jordan had been on a business trip driving his own car and hadn't been heard from in several days. The entire Jordan family was concerned.

The tension mounted for several weeks, then the shocking news hit the airwaves. First, a body was found in a creek. Then, shortly after, Mr. Jordan's car was located, and the body was identified as his. He had been shot to death. Later, two 18-year-old youths were arrested and charged with

his killing in a random robbery. The boys had come upon Mr. Jordan napping in his car on the side of a highway and had no idea who he was until they went through his belongings after killing him.

Michael and his family were devastated by the loss, and the nation shared their grief. Michael and his father had always been extremely close. They were best friends as well as father and son, and Mr. Jordan was a fixture at almost every Bulls' game.

The funeral for James Jordan was private, and aside from expressing his initial grief, Michael said very little to the press for the next several months. Then, on October 6, shortly before Bulls' training camp opened, Michael called a press conference and shocked the sporting world. He announced that he was retiring from basketball.

"I have nothing more to prove in basketball," he told the gathering. "I have no more challenges that I [feel] I could get motivated for. It doesn't have anything to do with my father's passing, or media pressure, or anything other than I had achieved everything in basketball I could. I felt it [is] time to call it a career.

"My father saw my last basketball game and that means a lot."

There was a feeling that Michael would change his mind, that his father's death was the real rea-

At a news conference on October 6, 1993, an emotional Michael Jordan announces his retirement from basketball. His wife, Juanita, is next to him.

son for his announcement. But when the Bulls opened training camp, reality set in. For the first time in a decade, Michael Jordan wasn't there. If he stayed retired, he would leave behind the highest career scoring average ever, both for the regular season (32.2) and the playoffs (34.7). Many still felt that he would be back, maybe after a year or two.

But the Bulls prepared to go on without him. Many reporters went to Scottie to ask about Michael.

"I'm sure Michael knows that physically he can still play the game," Scottie said. "But the question is: Does he still have any desire to play it? I guess this summer was very hard on him."

As for Scottie, he was suddenly the main man, and Coach Jackson reminded him of that as soon as camp opened. He pulled Scottie aside and said, "The saddle goes on your back. We're going to ride you."

Scottie was ready for the challenge, but he also warned people that he wasn't Michael Jordan. "I'll never be able to score like Michael, even if I tried," he said. "I'm not trying to be Michael. I don't need to be for this team to win. I can only be what I am."

The Bulls made one major addition in 1993–1994. They signed 6-foot-11-inch (210-centimeter) Toni Kukoc, who was from Croatia. Kukoc was one of the finest players in Europe and was expected to become an NBA star. But he wouldn't replace Michael. No one could. And Scottie Pippen would no longer be part of the best one-two punch in the game.

An ankle injury forced Scottie to miss a few games at the start of the season. When he returned, it took a few more games for him to get into top shape. By then, the team was struggling at 5–7, and people were saying that they couldn't win with-

out Michael. But a game with Phoenix on November 30 proved to be a turning point. In that game, Scottie had 29 points, with 11 rebounds and 6 assists, as the Bulls won 132–113.

From there, the team won 15 of its next 18, and began rolling once again. By January, the Bulls were in the race for the division title. That's when they were surprised again. Michael Jordan announced that he had signed a contract with the Chicago White Sox. Starting in the spring of 1994, he would play minor-league baseball with the hopes of becoming a major leaguer. Most experts felt that he was a longshot, at best. Michael hadn't played baseball since he was very young.

Michael began his baseball career quietly. He had some skills in the field and on the bases. But, like so many others who tried, he couldn't hit a curveball or adjust quickly enough to pitchers' changing speeds. He had been away from the game of baseball for too long, but he gave it a try.

Back on the hardwood, Scottie was putting together a fine season. No, he wasn't Michael—he couldn't explode for 50 points a game. But his all-around play was superb. He showed it in the mid-season All-Star Game by being named the game's Most Valuable Player. Then he returned to lead the Bulls to a 55–27 season. The team finished two games behind Atlanta in the division.

Scottie had averaged a career best 22 points for 72 games. He also had a career best 8.7 rebounds per contest, added 403 assists, and was second in the league with 2.93 steals per game. He would be named both a first team All-Star and All-Defensive first teamer. There was little doubt now about how good he had become.

In the playoffs, the Bulls wound up meeting the Knicks in the Eastern Conference final. The Knicks won the first two games in New York. Game three in Chicago came down to one shot with 1.8 seconds left, the Bulls trailing by one. When Coach Jackson diagrammed a play that would have Scottie decoy and Toni Kukoc take the final shot, Scottie refused to reenter the game. Kukoc went out to hit a long three-pointer to win it.

Like all great players, Scottie had wanted the ball in that situation. But later, he admitted that sitting out was wrong. "I put it behind me," he said. "I apologized to the team and to Phil Jackson. You always learn from mistakes. I just keep moving and try to do better."

It was a series that came down to a seventh and deciding game at Madison Square Garden. The Knicks won it, 87–77, ending the Bulls' championship run.

Some people thought that the Bulls would now begin to fade as a team. But no one knew then of

the drama that would take place toward the end of the 1994–1995 season, or that the next few years would see Scottie Pippen raise his game even more. Or that once again he would play alongside Michael Jordan to form the most exciting teammates in the game.

While Scottie was leading the Bulls to the Eastern Conference finals in 1994, Michael was still struggling in the minor leagues. Playing the outfield for the Class-A Birmingham (Alabama) Barons, he was hitting below .200. He would finish the season batting a less-than-great .202.

"It's been embarrassing, it's been frustrating, and it can make you mad," Michael said during the season. "I don't remember the last time I had all those feelings at once. And I've been working too hard at this to make myself look like a fool." Michael worked as hard as the teenage rookies. But it was soon apparent to veteran baseball people that Michael had virtually no chance to make it to the big leagues.

Although he gave it his all, Michael never quite cut it as a baseball player. With the 1994 players' strike looming on the horizon, Michael, in his Birmingham Barons uniform, shagged fly balls before a game against the Knoxville Smokies on August 10.

While the Bulls prepared for training camp, Michael returned to the Arizona Fall League to play baseball once again. At the same time, Scottie and the Bulls now had to prepare for life without Horace Grant. The star power forward had left the team and signed a free-agent contract with the Orlando Magic. The Bulls would be even more shorthanded.

Once again Scottie Pippen was playing brilliant basketball. Only now he must have felt the way Michael had early in his career—he just didn't have enough help. The Bulls were a winning team, but by a smaller margin than before. They were struggling just to stay above .500.

Scottie was a starter in the All-Star Game again, but was more concerned about his team. Then, shortly after the All-Star break in February, some happenings in baseball began catching the attention of the Bulls and their fans. The Major League Players' Association had gone on strike August 12, 1994, when they were unable to resolve their labor problems with the owners. The strike caused the cancellation of the balance of the 1994 baseball season, including the World Series, for the first time in history.

Now, with baseball's spring training approaching, the strike was still not settled. The owners were talking about using replacement players, or, in effect, strikebreakers. The major-league players

also asked the minor leaguers not to play their preseason exhibition games. Michael felt he had to respect the Players' Association's wishes. He had always backed the basketball players' union and wouldn't change now.

But he would also lose valuable time in his quest to make the White Sox. In early March, he suddenly left the White Sox training camp. He said he would not go to the big leagues as a replacement player. Since it still wasn't time to report to the Sox minor-league camp, Michael returned to Chicago. Next, he surprised everyone by joining in at several Bulls' practice sessions. Naturally, the rumor mill began churning.

On March 10, as the NBA season was in its final stages, Michael called a press conference and once again surprised everyone. Now he announced his retirement from baseball. Michael cited the continuing players' strike as the reason, saying it had impeded his development and that he was "no longer comfortable that there is meaningful opportunity to continue my improvement at a satisfactory pace."

But what next? Many felt that the strike had given Michael an "out," an opportunity to leave baseball gracefully. After all, his chances of making the majors at the age of 32 were remote. Yet he was certainly still young enough to return to basketball. But would he?

It didn't take long to learn the answer. On March 18, 1995, just eight days after retiring from baseball, Michael issued a written statement to the press. It consisted of just two words: *I'm back.*

At that late point in the season, the Bulls were just 34–31 with 17 games left. That night, the team would meet the Indiana Pacers at the Market Square Arena. All the excitement was created by the return of Michael Jordan. He came out on the court wearing number 45, which he had worn in baseball. He would explain that 23, his former number, was the number that his father had last seen him in. He didn't want to be seen in it again.

Michael was obviously rusty, and the team had to adjust to his return. But they made it close, losing to the Pacers in overtime, 103–96. Michael had 19 points, but hit just 7 of his 28 shots from the field. Scottie's brilliant play almost enabled the team to pull it out.

Soon, Michael was getting his court legs back. He won a game against Atlanta with a last-second buzzer-beater, scoring 32 points total. Against the Knicks at Madison Square Garden, he put on a vintage show, finishing with an amazing 55 points. As always, he said his ultimate goal was another championship.

The Bulls won 13 of their final 17 games with Michael in the lineup, finishing at 47–35. Michael averaged 26.9 points in his brief return. Maybe he

Reunited teammates Pippen and Jordan (wearing his new number, 45) return to the floor after a time-out in Michael's first game after coming out of retirement.

wasn't quite his old self, but Scottie Pippen was. Michael's teammate had turned in another all-star season.

Scottie averaged 21.4 points a game with a career best 639 rebounds. He led the league in steals and led the club in assists. Not surprisingly, he was a first team All-NBA selection and on the All-Defensive first team. In Michael's absence, he had become a fully recognized superstar of the game. Now they were teammates again, heading into the playoffs.

That's where the team stalled. In the first round they topped the Charlotte Hornets in four games, but in the Eastern Conference semifinals against Shaquille O'Neal and the Orlando Magic, they couldn't get it done. Orlando topped the Bulls in six games, ending their season. Michael had even tried to change his team's fortunes by going back to his old number 23. But the Magic were too strong.

Michael didn't waste much time announcing his intentions. He said he would be back for a full season in 1995–1996, with his goal being to help the Bulls win another championship. And this time he would be joined by Scottie Pippen, who had become an even more complete player in Michael's absence. The two teammates were about to show the entire basketball world just how good they could be together.

THE RECORD-SETTING BULLS

The Bulls made one major change before the new season began—they signed forward Dennis Rodman. Rodman was known as an outrageous personality. He had tattoos over much of his body. He changed the color of his hair nearly every night. His body was pierced for jewelry in various places. He was volatile and often unpredictable. But he was also the game's best rebounder, a great defensive player, and a ferocious competitor.

It was apparent from the outset of the 1995–1996 season that the Bulls were something special. Michael was back in full game shape; Scottie was better than ever; and Rodman was rebounding like a terror. Add some other solid players—

like center Luc Longley, guards Steve Kerr and Ron Harper, and center Bill Wennington—and the Bulls were obviously the team to beat.

But no one expected them to be quite as good as they were. When the Bulls rolled into Madison Square Garden for a late January game against the Knicks, they had amassed an incredible 34–3 record. They were dominating the NBA as no team had before, and were on pace to be the first team to win 70 games in a season. Many were wondering how they could be so dominant. After all, it was Michael's first full year after almost two years off. Rodman was a loose cannon. And Scottie couldn't play in the clutch.

It was that all three players had elevated their games. Despite his eccentricities, the nearly 35-year-old Rodman was in tremendous physical condition. He made every rebound a personal quest. And he knew how to upset his opponents psychologically. As usual, he was leading the league in rebounds.

Michael had made some subtle changes in his style. He didn't drive as much, or fly through the air with defenders chopping at him. He began leaning more on a fallaway jump shot that no one could defend. On occasion, he still drove to the basket and turned back the clock with his in-air moves. He was a smarter player and no one was better

with the game on the line. He hadn't lost his ability to take over a game offensively and make it all his own.

The thing that most seemed to take the Bulls to their elevated status, however, was the outstanding all-around play of Scottie Pippen. He had had nearly two years to hone his skills and forge his own personality when Michael was playing baseball. One writer said that for the first time Scottie always appeared "assured and settled," and that he finally seemed to be liberated playing beside Michael. In addition, he was finally being looked upon as what he is, not what he isn't. And what he is "is the top end-to-end performer in his sport."

Orlando Magic assistant coach Richie Adubato had this assessment of Scottie's skills: "He has the ability to press, play his man individually, double-team, rotate, block shots from behind, and just disrupt the whole offense. Sometimes, it seems as if there are three of him out there."

Early in the year, someone asked Michael if he still felt he was the best in the league. He answered quickly. "I'm not even the best player on this team."

Scottie's all-court game was simply devastating. Michael's all-court game was very close to being the same. The only difference defensively was that Scottie was a little bigger, enabling him to do more underneath the basket. Offensively, Michael

The 1995–1996 season saw Scottie emerge as one of the true superstars of basketball. His superior all-around play made him step out of Michael's shadow. In a 1996 playoff game, Scottie goes up for an easy two points.

was still capable of the big explosion—that would always set him apart from everyone else.

The winning Chicago combination rode it home to a record-setting season. They finished with an all-time mark of 72–10, an incredible record in a sport with such a long, grueling season. Michael won his eighth scoring title with a 30.4 average. Scottie averaged 19.4 points and put up his usual high numbers across the board. Both Michael and Scottie were first team All-NBA choices, while Rodman joined them on the All-Defensive first team. Michael was once again the league's Most Valuable Player, the fourth time he won the award.

In the playoffs, the Bulls continued to dominate. They swept Charlotte in three straight, then whipped the New York Knicks in five games. In the conference finals, the Bulls once again met Shaquille O'Neal and the Orlando Magic. This time it was sweet revenge. The Bulls' all-around game was too much for O'Neal, Penny Hardaway, and the fine Orlando team to overcome. The Bulls swept them in four straight.

In the fourth and final game, Michael erupted for 45 points, putting on an offensive show that reminded people of just how good he really was. The first to compliment Michael's effort was his teammate, Scottie Pippen. "[Michael] played the

way we needed him to play to walk out of here with a win," said Scottie, who had an off night shooting. "This is revenge for him to be able to prove he's still able to carry a team. I knew he had the rhythm and I kept trying to get him the ball. He kept making the shots for us."

In the finals, the Bulls had to meet the tough Seattle SuperSonics, who had won 64 games during the regular season. The Sonics were led by point guard Gary Payton and power forward Shawn Kemp, and were a very solid team. But it was hard to see how anyone could top the Bulls. According to Brian Hill, coach of the defeated Magic, Michael Jordan just wouldn't allow the Bulls to lose. "Frankly, I don't think Michael will be denied," Hill said. "I think this whole postseason is a testimony to his will."

There was no doubt that Michael was the game's fiercest competitor, as well as its most outstanding talent. He was still the greatest single offensive threat. But team defense also won for the Bulls, and when talking about defense, Michael and Scottie were always mentioned in the same breath.

"Jordan and Pippen [are] the leaders of a nasty, attack-dog defense that took the heart, spirit, and life out of the opposition all season," one writer explained. "Not once have Michael or Scottie fouled

out of a game. In the playoffs, Jordan and Pippen have continued their aggressive defensive assaults."

As his team sat poised on the brink of another title, Michael thought about what motivated him as a player. "It would be very, very gratifying [to win again as] a tribute to my father and the motivation he has provided," Michael said. "Even though he hasn't been around, that's part of my motivation every day, to go out and make him proud of what I've done."

The series against the Sonics was almost anticlimactic. The Bulls won the first three games, although it wasn't easy. Scottie still wasn't playing at 100 percent physically, and some of the other veterans were tired. Seattle rallied to take the fourth and fifth games before the Bulls closed it out in six for their fourth championship in six years, winning the finale 87–75. For Michael and Scottie, this was probably the sweetest one of all. Asked if he would have returned to the Bulls had Scottie not been there, Michael gave a quick answer. "No, definitely no. That's how much I respect Scottie Pippen."

The 1996–1997 season almost looked like a carbon copy of the year before. After all, the Bulls finished just three games behind their record-setting pace of 1995–1996. They were 69–13, the best record in the league once again. Michael won

yet another scoring title with a 29.6 average. Scottie averaged 20.2 points. Both players were in all 82 games.

But there were problems beneath the surface. Dennis Rodman had an erratic year. While he won the rebounding title with an impressive 16.1 per game, he played in only 55 contests. There were injuries, ejections, and suspensions. Rodman sometimes seemed more concerned with promoting his outrageous image rather than playing basketball.

In addition, Scottie was unhappy about his contract, which was paying him a lot less than players who didn't have his talent. Phil Jackson said that he didn't know if he would be returning as coach. And there was talk about breaking up the aging team and rebuilding.

Yet with Michael and Scottie still working together, the Bulls continued to dominate. When the NBA chose its 50 greatest all-time players, both were among the league's elite. After the regular season, Michael was on the All-NBA first team, while Scottie made the second. And when Utah's Karl Malone was named the league's Most Valuable Player by a narrow margin over Michael, even he seemed surprised. "I thank Michael for letting me borrow [the award] for one year," he said.

Coming into the playoffs, the Bulls were favorites. But unlike the year before, there was a feeling

that they could be beaten. Scottie had a soft-tissue injury in his foot that was becoming increasingly painful. Michael was healthy; but no one knew how the unpredictable Rodman would respond.

But sure enough, when just two teams remained, the Bulls were there to defend their title. Meeting them in the finals were Karl Malone and the Utah Jazz, a team that had won 64 games in the regular season. And once again, whenever anyone talked about the Bulls in the finals, the names of Jordan and Pippen were always linked.

Coach Jackson talked about the psychological advantage that Jordan and Pippen had over their opponents. "I think [that in Michael] we carry probably one of the best psychological players that's ever played the game," said the coach. "Scottie has gotten to that level, too, where they know how to attack. They've got great presence on the floor. They've got poise and confidence that can be overwhelming in some areas."

The first game was close all the way. As had happened so many times before, Michael took it on his shoulders and hit a 21-foot jump shot at the buzzer to give the Bulls an 84–82 victory. Michael finished with 31 points. Scottie chipped in with 27 points and grabbed 9 rebounds—all with the sore foot. The great one-two punch had prevailed again.

Michael and Scottie give a high-five after leading the Bulls to victory over the Atlanta Hawks in the 1997 playoffs. The Bulls went on to win the series with Atlanta and to top the Utah Jazz to win the championship.

Chicago also won the second game before the Jazz battled back and won the third and fourth to tie the series. Michael simply looked at it as another challenge. "This situation we're in may be exactly what we need," he said. "It's a great challenge and no one said this was going to be easy. We haven't been put in this position for a long time, and that's fun to me."

Michael was about to go out and put on one of the most courageous performances of his long career. Before the game, Michael had come down with the flu. He was vomiting almost until game time, yet came out on the court with his teammates. Then he played his heart out. Several times, he looked to be on the brink of collapse, but he found the strength from some place deep inside him to continue.

With the other Bulls not shooting well, the team needed Michael to come up big. With 25 seconds left, he hit a huge three-pointer that gave his team a 90–88 victory. When the game was over, he needed an IV to put fluids into his dehydrated body. Yet he had scored 38 points in a truly incredible performance.

"Sometimes you've got to come out and do what you've got to do," he said. "We wanted it real bad and I, as a leader, had to do my best, and hopefully the team would rally around me."

They did. And in the sixth game they closed out the series for the team's fifth title in seven years. And when Michael was presented the finals' Most Valuable Player award, he called Scottie over to help him hold it aloft.

Michael might have been the greatest, but he knew that his team would never have won five championships had it not been for his outstanding teammate.

When the 1996–1997 season ended, there were immediate questions. Would the team be disbanded? After all, the Bulls were now the oldest team in the league. But they were also still the best. Michael made his feelings known quickly. "We're the champions," he said. "We should be given every chance to defend our title until someone beats us."

Why would management even consider breaking up a team like the Bulls? Some of it had to do with a personality conflict. It was no secret that management wanted a new coach. Phil Jackson had had some difficult contract negotiations with the team. He had talked about going elsewhere, or

simply sitting out a year or two. Once again, he didn't know if he'd be back in 1997–1998.

Dennis Rodman was another question. He had looked disinterested for much of the past season. Even though he won another rebounding title, his teammates lost some confidence in him because of his unpredictable behavior. In addition, he had missed some 27 games for various reasons. He was also 36 years old. Word was that the team didn't want him back.

And that left the two great teammates—Jordan and Pippen. Those who knew Michael best said that he was enjoying the game as never before. He would be 35 years old in February 1998, but was still a dominant player. He was among the wealthiest athletes in the world, having just finished a one-year, $30 million contract. That was well deserved, because he generated huge amounts of money for the team and the league.

His many off-court endorsements, commercials, and his movie work netted him even more money than his basketball contract. Money was not a concern for Michael. He had made it clear on a number of occasions that if Coach Jackson or Scottie did not return to the team, he would retire. He wanted to keep the team intact.

For Scottie, the problem *was* money. He had signed a long-term contract a number of years ear-

lier that had quickly become obsolete. He was earning about $3 million a year. That is certainly a tidy sum, but when players of obviously lesser talent were earning two or three times as much, it rankled him. And the Bulls hadn't moved to renegotiate his contract, which had one more year to run. It had gotten so bad that Scottie and GM Jerry Krause rarely spoke, despite the glowing things the general manager had said about Scottie over the years.

Scottie would be 32 years old at the beginning of the 1997–1998 season. He was still at the top of his game. There was no reason to think he still wouldn't command a much bigger contract once he became a free agent at the end of the season. Of course, there was also a chance that the Bulls would trade him, which would be a gamble because it might force Michael to retire.

The other problem was Scottie's foot, the one that had troubled him so much in the playoffs. He thought rest would be the answer. But whenever he worked out, the pain returned. Finally, he had no choice but to undergo surgery. The operation took place in October 1997. It would cause him to miss the first few months of the new season, and he was projected to return in mid-January.

Finally, the pieces began falling into place for the Bulls. Coach Jackson signed a one-year contract. Michael signed another huge one-year deal,

The early part of the 1997–1998 season was full of tension for the Bulls. A foot injury that would require surgery sidelined Scottie, and there was talk that he was dissatisfied with his contract and wanted to leave the team. Would this season be the last for the two greatest teammates the sport of basketball had ever known?

estimated at about $33 million. Scottie, of course, was still under contract. Then, shortly before the season began, the team re-signed Dennis Rodman, at Michael's urging.

Without Scottie, however, the team struggled in the early going. But soon a rededicated Rodman was leading the NBA in rebounding, and Toni

Kukoc, filling in at small forward to Scottie, was also playing very well.

Michael was up to his old tricks. On December 30, he set a new record by scoring in double figures in his 788th-straight game. The old mark had been held by the legendary Kareem Abdul-Jabbar. About the same time, he had a run of four games in which he topped the 40-point mark three times. There was no doubt that he could still do it better than anyone.

Though Scottie still wasn't happy with his contract and had said he might not play for the Bulls again, he set a target date to return in January 1998, citing loyalty to his teammates as his overriding motivation. "I've got a good relationship with my teammates," he said. "They know I'm not going to leave them hanging."

Scottie returned on Saturday, January 10, after missing the first 35 games of the season. Playing against the Golden State Warriors, he scored 14 points, and had 4 rebounds and 5 assists in 31 minutes of action. The Bulls won the game 87–82, running their record to 25–11, and putting them squarely in line for a third straight championship, which would be their sixth in eight years.

It took several games for Scottie to shake off the rust, but soon he was again playing at an all-star level. "Everyone kind of put us behind the

eight ball early on because of the absence of Scottie," Michael said. "But we've survived that. I think what the rest of the teams are starting to see is that it's not going to be an easy fight to take what we have. We're going to fight for every little inch, every player on this team, to defend what is ours."

The brilliant teammates were back together and both knew that the Bulls would be tough to beat. After all, with Michael Jordan and Scottie Pippen, the Bulls had their formula for success, a formula that propelled them to a third straight championship in 1998.

As they had in 1997, the Bulls defeated the Utah Jazz in the finals, winning in six games. Michael was brilliant as usual, winning the MVP Award and scoring 45 points in the final game. Scottie had an outstanding series as well, though a back injury forced him to play the last two games with severe pain. When it was over, the Bulls had their sixth championship in eight years.

Michael continued to leave an incredible mark on the NBA and on the entire sports world. Early in the season he became the league's third all-time scorer, trailing only Kareem Abdul-Jabbar and Wilt Chamberlain. He also introduced Jordan Brand, a line of sports apparel and athletic shoes. Always an astute businessman, Michael seemed to be pre-

paring for life after basketball, though he continued to play at an all-world level.

Scottie Pippen has never done things in quite the same way as his more illustrious teammate. Always more of a private person than Michael, Scottie shunned the limelight early in his career. Perhaps the two years that Michael was gone enabled him to emerge as a personality in his own right. He now has considerable commercial endorsements, is a highly visible personality, and is fully recognized for the great player he has become.

Both Michael and Scottie have used their celebrity status to do a considerable amount of charity work, organizing events to benefit children and various charitable organizations. Scottie has never forgotten his hometown, raising money and donating considerable sums of his own money to help renovate a public park and set up other sports facilities for kids. People entering Hamburg, Arkansas, from any direction will see a sign that reads: WELCOME. YOU ARE NOW ENTERING SCOTTIE PIPPEN COUNTRY. HAMBURG, ARKANSAS.

Michael Jordan has become an American icon. His feature film *Space Jam* was a partially animated comedy for children and was a big hit. It's also nearly impossible to watch an evening of television without seeing Michael appear as a spokesman for one or more products.

No one will argue the fact that Michael is the single greatest talent ever to play the game of basketball. But he's also a player who has dug deep within himself to maximize his awesome talent. No challenge is too large; no goal too high. There has probably never been a more competitive athlete in any sport.

Scottie Pippen traveled a different road. As a college freshman, Michael Jordan was hitting a shot that brought his team a national championship. As a college freshman, Scottie was handing out towels as team manager. He had a long way to travel in a short time. His basketball life changed when he met Michael. Had he not joined a team with such a high-profile player, the pressure to excel might have been too great. With Michael already there, he was able to develop his game without the need to be an instant star.

Scottie found many of the same qualities that made Michael so great. Michael Jordan and Scottie Pippen were two parts of the same equation, a pair of players who could beat their opponents in so many different ways. Singularly, each would still have been a great ballplayer. Together, they became arguably the most devastating pair of teammates ever to grace the hardwood.